Contents

season

A **season** is a time of year.

spring

summer

4

Each season has different weather.

autumn

winter

5

spring

Spring is a season.

Sue Barraclough

WAYLAND

First published in 2007 by Wayland

This paperback edition published in 2011 by Wayland

Wayland
338 Euston Road
London NW1 3BH

Wayland Australia
Level 17/207 Kent Street
Sydney, NSW 2000

Design: Natascha Frensch
Typography: Natascha Frensch
Read Regular (European Community Design Registration 2003)
Read Regular and Read Xheavy copyright © Natascha Frensch 2001-2006

Editor: Joyce Bentley
Picture research: Sue Barraclough

ISBN 978 07502 6527 0

Printed in China

Wayland is a division of Hachette Children's Books, an Hachette UK Company.
www.hachette.co.uk
Acknowledgements: Cover © image100/Corbis; p 1,12 & 22 © Comstock/Corbis; pp 2-3 © Dietrich Rose/
zefa/Corbis; pp 4-5 Kathy Collins/Photographer's Choice/Getty; pp 6-7 & 22 © Robert Llewellyn/zefa/Corbis;
pp 8-9 © image100/Corbis; p 11 & 22 © Bloomimage/Corbis; p13 & 22 Anne Ackerman/Taxi/Getty; p15
Ian Boddy, Science Photo Library; p16 Simon Wilkinson/Iconica/Getty; p17 Superstudio/Taxi/Getty; pp 16-17
© Richard Hamilton Smith/Corbis; pp 20-21 © Craig Tuttle/Corbis

New green leaves and flowers grow.

summer

Summer is a season.

We play outside in warm weather.

sky

The **sky** is blue in summer.

Butterflies fly from flower to flower.

autumn

Autumn is a season.

Some leaves change colour.

windy

Autumn is **windy**.

Windy weather is good for flying a kite.

leaves

In autumn, **leaves** fall.

This girl plays in the **leaves**.

winter

Winter is a season.

Many trees have no leaves.

cold

Winter is **cold**.

We wear warm clothes in winter.

snow

In winter, it can **snow**.

Playing in the snow is fun!

rainbow

We see **rainbows** in all seasons.

Sunshine and rain make a **rainbow** of many colours.

Picture quiz

Can you find these things in the book?

kite

flowers

butterfly

leaves

What pages are they on?

Index quiz

The index is on page 24.
Use the index and pictures
to answer these questions.

1. Which pages show **snow**?
   How many sledges can you count?

2. Which pages show summer is **warm**?
   How many children are playing?

3. Which pages show a **rainbow**?
   What two things make a rainbow?

4. Which page shows winter is **cold**?
   How many woolly hats can you see?

Index

Answers

Picture quiz: The kite is on page 13. The flowers are on page 7. The butterfly is on page 11. The leaves are on page 12.
Index quiz: 1. Page 18-19, three; 2. Page 9-10, three; 3. Page 20-21, sun and rain; 4. Page 17, one.

"I want to go to Seal Island," said Peter.

"The sea is dangerous," said Granny.

"I'll walk across the sands when the tide is out."

"The sands are dangerous," said Granny. "They'll suck you in if you don't tread carefully."

"But the oysterman knows a safe way across the sands," said Peter. "He has oysterbeds on Seal Island."

"Stay away from the oysterman and that lazy wife of his," said Granny. "Don't try to follow him."

At low tide Peter often watched the oysterman go carefully over the sands, leaving a line of sticks to mark his way.

SELKIE

A Scottis

Gillian McC

troika bo

www.troikabook

F ar away, on the edge of the sea, a boy named Peter lived with his granny.
At high tide, the sea stretched from their cottage to Seal Island. But at
low tide, the sea drew back and uncovered a long stretch of sand.

"Stay away from Seal Island," Peter's granny said.
But the cries of the seals on the wind kept calling Peter.

Before high tide, the oysterman returned with a sackful of oysters to sell. Peter watched him lifting his sticks, one by one, with the sea coming in behind him.

One day, when Granny was not looking, Peter ran to the cottage where the oysterman lived with his wife. Peter found him outside mending nets and chanting:

"One day I'll catch the Selkie.
Selkie, you will help me
Learn the language of the sea.
One day I'll catch the Selkie.
Selkie, you will help me
Gather riches from the sea."

"Please, Mr Oysterman," said Peter, "will you show me the way over the sands to Seal Island?"

The oysterman jumped up and roared, "Stay away from Seal Island, boy!" and threw his net at Peter, but only caught Peter's hat. Peter ran back to his granny.

Granny was angry. "Next time it won't just be a hat caught in the oysterman's net..."

"He wants to catch a Selkie," Peter said. "What's a Selkie, Granny?"

"A Selkie is a seal that turns into a girl when she takes her seal skin off. A Selkie knows the secret language of the sea," Granny replied.

The next day, Peter slipped out to look for his hat. It was low tide and he saw the oysterman far out on the sands on his way to Seal Island. The path of sticks started from the oysterman's cottage.

Peter thought, "If I follow the sticks, then I can teach myself the safe way over the sands." He set out carefully.

When he reached Seal Island, Peter saw the oysterman bent over his oysterbeds.

Peter kept out of sight. Round the other side of the island, he came upon a flock of seals on the rocks. Suddenly Peter heard splashing coming from a pool.

Peter saw a beautiful seal caught in one of the oysterman's nets.

As he struggled to free the seal, her skin slipped off and a young girl stood there.

Peter gasped, "You must be a Selkie!"

The girl smiled at him. "Yes I am," she said. "How can I thank you for setting me free?"

Just then, Peter felt the sea lap over the top of his boot. "The tide's coming in!" he cried. "Quick! I must cross the sands while the oysterman's sticks are still there."

But when he ran to the other side of the island, he saw the sea stretching over the sands and, in the distance, the oysterman lifting his last stick.

"You must stay on Seal Island until the tide goes out again," said Selkie. Peter knew he had hours to wait and that his granny would be worried.

"Dear friend," said Selkie, "you set me free and now I will begin to teach you the secret language of the sea."

She taught Peter to hear the voices of the fish, to see the patterns of the waves and to know the words of the wind. The hours went by and soon the tide began going out again.

Then Peter told Selkie, "The oysterman thinks that learning the language of the sea will make him rich."

Selkie laughed. "A greedy man can never learn the language of the sea," she said.

Suddenly, there was the oysterman with his net.

"GOT YOU!"

Selkie tried to put on her seal skin and escape, but the oysterman grabbed the skin with one hand and held the net firmly in the other.

As the oysterman dragged
Selkie over the sands, Peter
heard his chant:

"Today I caught you, Selkie.
Selkie, you will help me
Learn the language of the sea.
Today I caught you, Selkie.
Selkie, you will help me
Gather riches from the sea."

Peter followed the oysterman
ashore.

The oysterman took Selkie into his cottage to show his wife. Peter crept close and peered through the window.

He saw the oysterman's wife dressing Selkie in an old petticoat. He saw the oysterman putting something up into the rafters.

When Peter got home, his granny sent him straight to bed. But he couldn't sleep.

He was worried about Selkie. He had to help her get back to Seal Island and he was trying to remember the pattern of the sticks in the sand.

Selkie could not sleep, either. The seals were calling her.

She saw the sea stretching out to the island and she knew she could not swim there without her seal skin.

Later, she saw the sands stretching out to the island and she knew she could not walk there without the oysterman's sticks to guide her.

The next day, Peter went to the oysterman's cottage. He saw the oysterman loading his cart with oysters to sell. He heard him grumbling about his lazy wife, who never got up in the mornings.

Peter knew he would be gone all day.

Inside the cottage Selkie sat weeping, a bowl of porridge the oysterman had given her untouched.

In her bed, the oysterman's wife snored. Peter crept in. "Quick! Follow me across the sands to Seal Island while the tide is out. I've remembered the way."

"But my seal skin," sobbed Selkie. "I cannot swim with the seals without it."

They searched everywhere in the cottage. It was nowhere to be found. Then Peter remembered seeing the oysterman reaching up into the rafters. And there was the seal skin!

Taking the oysterman's sticks and placing them in the pattern he remembered, Peter led the way safely over the sands.

They reached the island, and Peter turned to Selkie, but she had already put on her seal skin. Instead of a girl, a beautiful seal was sliding down to the water's edge.

As she dived in, Peter heard her call out goodbye to him in the secret language of the sea. Peter felt sad. For a long time he watched Selkie swimming with the seals.

By the time Peter turned to go back, darkness was falling. The tide was coming in fast. He saw a light moving along the far shore. It was the oysterman returning home. Peter set off.

The sea swirled round his ankles, then his knees, then his chest. But he was not afraid because the patterns of the waves, the voices of the fish and the words of the wind led him safely back to shore.

As Peter came out of the water, he saw the oysterman raging outside his cottage:

"I have lost my precious Selkie.
Now she'll never help me
Gather riches from the sea!"

Then Peter shouted,

"Dear Selkie, you have taught me,
Better than all its riches,
The secret language of the sea."

As the wind carried Peter's cry out to sea, a seal's head slipped silently under the waves.

Published by troika books

First published by Doubleday 1999
This edition published 2015

1 2 3 4 5 6 7 8 9 10

Text and illustrations copyright © Gillian McClure 1999
The moral rights of the author/illustrator have been asserted

Design: Lisa Kirkham and Louise Millar

A CIP catalogue record for this book is available from the British Library

ISBN 978-1-909991-26-2

Printed in China

Troika Books
Well House, Green Lane, Ardleigh CO7 7PD

www.troikabooks.com